MASTERPIECE

OLUBUNMI ALADE

God's Masterpiece
Copyright © 2022 by Olubunmi Alade

Published by
Sophos Books
163 Warbank Crescent
Croydon
CR0 0AZ

All scriptures, unless otherwise stated. are taken from the New King James Version of the Bible.

ISBN 978-1-905669-73-8

Cover design by Icon Media
Printed in the United Kingdom

Contents

DEDICATION

I dedicate this book first to my Lord and Saviour Jesus Christ who paid the price for my redemption.

To those who have the inherited disease called Sickle-Cell Anaemia and going through crises and challenges of life.

To my dear Mother in the Lord, Rev. Omome Udaze, for her prayers and encouragement during my early years in ministry and marriage.

Finally, to my late parents, Chief Emmanuel Oladipo Osunsedo and Chief (Mrs) Mercy Folashade Osunsedo (nee Ogunseinde), for their investment into my life.

ACKNOWLEDGMENTS

My thanks, praises, and adoration to the Holy Trinity for keeping me safe and sound to write this book.

I am also grateful to my wonderful companion and husband, Elder Michael Akinlolu Alade, who stood by me through my health challenges. I say thank you very much for supporting this project, and for your belief in me that I can document this true story of my life.

To my dear Pastor and friend, Layo Segun, of Great Beauty Tabernacle, who took it upon herself to read through the manuscript, making various corrections. Thank you for your inspiring words, which motivated me at every step. God will uphold you and enable you to fulfil your destiny by the power of the Holy Spirit.

I say a big thank you to my dear children, Emmanuel, Mary, and Yan, for their support and encouragement, even when I had to ask for their assistance at odd times.

My thanks and appreciation go to my uncle, Dr. Tunji Ogunseinde, who encouraged me to write this book. God bless you Sir.

Finally, I cannot end this page without acknowledging Dr. R. Amos of Homerton University Hospital. You are a very unique doctor. You stood by me whenever I needed your help. Thank you. Also, to the team of the Medical Day Unit, the other doctors, and nurses, I say "Thank you! God bless you all."

FOREWORD

Bunmi Alade has authored a must-read, powerful book full of information for those who are going through difficult patches in life, and for those who are supporting them. She takes readers on her rough, yet rewarding and exciting journey with sickle cell anaemia and brings them into her present grateful moment anchored on her faith in Christ Jesus, ending with a powerful call to action.

God's Masterpiece is a remarkable tale well told by a writer who blends life experience and faith. I held this profound and courageous book to my heart and was reminded of life's frail wonder.

'Bunmi Alade wants to equip you with a new way of coping with life challenges, whether you have human support or not. This book is highly recommended!

'Layo Segun,
Transformational Leader, Speaker, Author,
and Senior Pastor, Great Beauty Tabernacle

PREFACE

This is a story about my life. The Lord knew me before He formed me in my mother's womb. He set me apart and appointed me as His minister before I was born (Jeremiah 1:5). Yes, despite my battles with sickle cell anaemia, God created me for a purpose.

Sickle cell anaemia is a serious, inherited blood disorder, where the red blood cells that carry oxygen around the body develop an abnormal shape, like a banana. It causes constant excruciating pain in the body. Although I was born with this rare blood disorder, I still give glory to the Almighty God who has kept me alive and helped me to live a normal life. He alone deserves all praise and adoration.

Many people thought I would not live up to eighteen years of age, but here I am today, gradually approaching seventy! Others thought I would not get married, but God has sustained my marriage of over thirty-six years. I am blessed with a caring husband, children, and a grandchild, with more on the way in Jesus Christ name. This is not by power nor by might, but by His precious blood. Hallelujah!

I employ all readers of this book who have sickle cell anaemia not to feel sorrowful or engage in pitiful attitude, instead, encourage yourself within, think positively about life, and explore areas where you can help other people. The word of God says, "I CAN DO ALL THINGS THROUGH CHRIST THAT GIVES ME STRENGTH'!

CHAPTER 1
Introduction

Dear reader, welcome to this journey of revelation, which will unveil the magnitude of God's grace and mercy upon my life. I never thought I would still be alive today, but I am grateful to God, who kept me alive to author this book. I also appreciate him for bringing caring and loving people on my path.

I was born over sixty years at the Charing Cross hospital, United Kingdom. My parents, Chief and Chief (Mrs) Osunsedo, were studying in the UK during my birth. While I was young, they decided to send me to Lagos, Nigeria via my mother's eldest sister. Prior to this period, my parents had an unpleasant experience. Their first male child died due to circumstances beyond their control in the United Kingdom.

My parents named me Oluwabunmi, Oluwafunmilayo, Ayodeji (meaning the Lord gift; the Lord has given me joy, and my joy has doubled). One of the reasons they gave me these names was to thank God that my father eventually passed his final pharmacy examination after a few attempts (my mother told me).

In Lagos, my mother's eldest sister safely handed me over to my paternal grandparents. My grandparents took care of me until I was around five years old. I could recall vividly that there were other children in that house. Some were my age mates while others were older than me. We were cousins, and we played together in the compound, which was large enough for us to run around. Some of the games we played include "Ring-a-ring-a-roses, a pocket full of roses," "ten ten", "who is in the garden", and "hide and seek." During this period, I doubt I would have recognised my parents if I had met them on the road. But I enjoyed genuine love from my grandmother.

Five years later, my parents returned to Nigeria and I now had a baby sister I could play with. Although I was glad to be living with my parents now even though I could not relate to them as I related to my grandparents. There seemed to be an emotional distance between my mother and me. I had become so attached to my grandmother that the bond between us was synonymous with the bond between a child and a mother. I later adjusted and accepted my mother after several rounds of pampering. The dynamics of this new development was that my grandmother was living with us. Hence I always clung to my grandmother, especially whenever my mother wanted to smack me for being naughty.

An incident happened after my eighth birthday. I collapsed as I was getting ready for school. I was rushed to the Lagos University Teaching Hospital (LUTH) on that fateful day. My mother immediately contacted her brother, Dr T. Ogunseinde, a medical doctor at LUTH. After several tests, my parents received the news about my health status. I had a rare medical condition called Sickle cell anaemia.

At the time of the diagnosis, I was attending Mainland Preparatory Primary School at Ebute-Metta. Whenever I felt sick, the pain would weaken me. I looked very sickly yet, each time, God helped me through the crisis. He also strengthened my parents, who were always there to administer the prescribed medications.

I want you to know that no matter what you are going through in life, be reassured that God knows about your situation. He is always mindful of you because you are precious to Him and He will take good care of you. Therefore, do not allow your present situation to jeopardise your future. The tension, difficulties or crisis you face will eventually end in Jesus' name. Amen.

CHAPTER 2

What Is Sickle Cell Anaemia?

Sickle cell anaemia is an inherited genetic blood disorder. It occurs when the red blood cells, usually soft and round, have a sickle shape. My genotype is SS. This means both my father and mother's genotype is AS. Among my siblings, I am the only child with the SS genotype and as such, I was diagnosed with Sickle cell disease. Sickle cell disease is common among people from sub-Saharan Africa, India, Saudi Arabia and Mediterranean countries.

There are diverse types of Sickle cell diseases, such as Sickle Cell Anaemia (SS), Sickle Cell + C Haemoglobin (S+C) and Sickle Cell + Beta-Thalassemia.

This book will focus on the area of my diagnosis and how it affected my life. At this juncture, I want to restate my gratitude to God for His grace that enables me to do all things. If not for His mercy, I would not be alive today to author this book.

The people who inherit one sickle cell gene and one normal gene have sickle cell trait (SCT), which is referred to as AS. AS is a healthy carrier condition. Most people with this condition do not have any of the symptoms of sickle cell disease, but they can pass the trait to their children, who may live a normal life with no life-threatening pains.

Figure 1

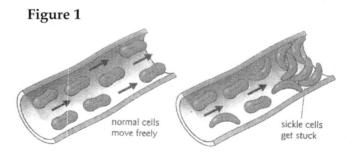

(Information from NHS Trust: Homerton University Hospital)

The red blood cells in the body take in oxygen from the air we breathe through our lungs to all parts of the body. Oxygen carries the red blood cells by a substance called haemoglobin A, a normal red blood cell, which is usually round, soft and can squeeze through tiny blood vessels. Typically, red blood cells live for about 120 days before new ones replace them. But people with sickle cell conditions have 'haemoglobin S' (S stands for sickle). Their red blood cells are stiff, distorted like a banana shape, making the cells difficult to pass through the blood vessels. These blood cells live for about 16 days, and the deformed shape often blocks the cells from flowing freely to other parts of the body, thereby causing complications and severe pains in different parts of the patient's body (see diagram above).

In another instance, when one parent is SS, and the other has AA genotype, each time they have a child, the haemoglobin type will only have an AS trait, which is not a disease. On the other hand, if one of the parents has SS and the other has an AS genotype, there is one in four chances that one of their children will inherit the Sickle Cell Anaemia (SS) and a fifty per cent chance of sickle cell trait.

Diagram A: These parents are AA & SS. They can produce offspring with AS, which does not have the sickle cell disease (SS).

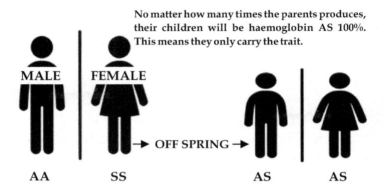

No matter how many times the parents produces, their children will be haemoglobin AS 100%. This means they only carry the trait.

Diagram B: These parents are AS & AS. There is a probability that the couple may have one or two children with sickle-cell and normal cells.

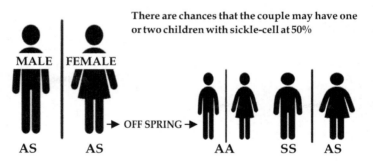

There are chances that the couple may have one or two children with sickle-cell at 50%

(Note: information from NHS Foundation Trust, Homerton University Hospital)

From the medical perspective, the red blood cells are destroyed rapidly in the body of people with the disease, causing anaemia, jaundice, and gallstones. Figure 1 shows how the sickle-shaped red blood cells block the flow of blood passing through vessels. Consequently, this blockage results in acute chest pain and pain episodes in the arms and joints. Prolonged pain may also occur in the abdomen, leading to stroke and priapism (painful erection in men). The blockage can also damage vital organs like the spleen, kidneys, liver and even the eyes (which may lead to blindness). Damage to the spleen also makes the patient, especially children, vulnerable to bacterial infections.

"fear not, for I am with you; be not dismayed, for I am your God; I will strengthen you, I will help you, I will uphold you with my righteous right hand."
Isaiah 41:10

CHAPTER 3
Effects And How To Adjust

People with sickle cell disease must manage their health from the early stage. When the disease is diagnosed early, it becomes easier to monitor it regularly with penicillin prophylaxis, vaccination against pneumococcus bacteria and folic acid supplement.

In a situation where the pain becomes severe, and some complications arise, the patient undergoes pain management, intravenous fluid, blood transfusion and surgery. Patients with the chronic disease must be monitored and managed with a programme of care.

The latest drug for treating sickle cell disease is

Hydroxyurea. It makes the red blood cells bigger, rounder and makes them less likely to turn into a sickle shape. Medical research has shown that Hydroxyurea reduces severe pain, acute chest pain and the need for blood transfusions in patients.

From experience, I have learnt to make some lifestyle changes and how to avoid certain habits. The sickle cell condition is painful, unpleasant, and demoralising, but we should trust that by God's grace, we will live long, achieve our goals, and succeed if we believe in the name of Jesus. Do not allow the situation to hinder you from fulfilling God's purpose for your life. Work hard and never take your eyes from God.

If you have been diagnosed with the sickle cell disease (SCD), observe the following:

1. Drink plenty of water and fluids every day, not just a glass but litres of water. You should also note that alcohol dehydrates, so apply wisdom when taking alcohol.

2. Keep your body warm during cold weather, either during the rainy season or winter.

3. Keep your home warm. Avoid sudden temperature changes. Do not stay too long in the water when swimming or in an air-

conditioned room. Wear warm clothing during cold weather.

4. If you exercise, avoid getting wet because if the water settles on your body for too long, it can affect your bones afterwards.

5. Be aware of your limitations. Get enough rest and relax when your body needs it.

6. Avoid being anxious; it will only trigger the crisis.

7. Avoid smoking or inhaling smoke. It will affect the lungs in the future.

8. Regularly attend your medical appointments with your doctor.

9. When you are in pain, do something to distract your mind from it. For example, you can read interesting novels or magazines, watch exciting programmes on the television, enjoy the company of your loved ones or listen to music.

10. Being a child of God, you must be prayerful. Listen to encouraging tapes and messages, and avoid negative statements at all cost.

11. When you are in a pain-free zone, do light exercises.

12. Eat healthy meals such as bran flakes cereal, plenty of fibre and fruits.

13. Mackerel fish is perfect. Some say it is a poor man's fish, but it is suitable for people diagnosed with sickle cell disease.

According to a survey, many people with sickle cell disease were not diagnosed at birth. For some, the symptoms will manifest a few years after birth. However, with technological advances and medical awareness, the disease can be detected from the womb after various tests have been carried out.

Sickle cell anaemia varies among individuals. Research has shown that cold environments, sudden weather changes, worries and stressful situations can trigger a crisis. In infants, lack of adequate knowledge may prevent parents or guardians from avoiding habits that may trigger pain episodes. Some patients who survived up to the age of forty said the pain reduced, while it is not so in others as they must go through blood transfusion depending on the severity.

In addition, as people with sickle cell anaemia grow, they learn to focus on getting better quickly, unlike many youths who take their health with levity and are more prone to visiting the hospitals. From the findings, some patients from a tender age do not have spleens. Likewise, some patients have damaged eyesight, but with regular intake of antibiotics, close observation and monitoring by doctors, some survive and live up to eighty years or more.

The survey, conducted in the United Kingdom, revealed that extra expenses were needed to heat the home to keep the house warm.

"Therefore do not worry about
tomorrow, for tomorrow will worry
about itself. Each day has enough
trouble of its own."
Matthew 6:34

CHAPTER 4
Life As An Adolescent

When I was ten years old, my parents gave birth to a bouncing baby boy. My mother was thrilled because, according to African tradition and beliefs in those days, a male child is superior to a female child. Many families believe that the female child always ends up in her husband's house, but the son will always be the heir. A boy child often makes the woman proud, and members of the husband's family hold the mother in high esteem in Yoruba culture. This explains why my mother was happy. And my beloved brother became the apple of her eye.

I later left the primary school at Ebute-Metta,

and I was registered at Corona School, Victoria Island, with my siblings. My parents did this to make life comfortable for us, and the Lord blessed the work of their hands.

After my primary education, I attended Girls Secondary Grammar School in Bariga, Lagos as a boarding student. It still amazes me that my parents could allow me to live outside the home where they could not monitor my medical condition.

My life at the hostel was short-lived due to my medical condition. The School Prefect always rang the bell for students to wake up by 5 am every day. We had morning hymnal songs and prayers every day, after which we had to fetch water at the well in the school compound. We would have breakfast and attend classes by 9 am with the day students. This was the day-to-day routine for the boarding students. However, my health condition would not allow me to stay long in the hostel. It was difficult for me to adjust to such a harsh environment.

The only option I had was to bathe with cold water. Secondly, the bathroom was like a shed and could only contain twenty students at a time. To avoid being late for classes, some girls would hang around the shed to bathe before daylight. Bathing with cold water was a tough and unpleasant experience for me. It resulted in uncontrollable pain. The principal informed my parents to get medical permission that I needed hot water to bathe. Permission was granted – hurray! You would think this would have made things easier for me and reduced the painful ordeal, but alas, it wasn't. After the morning prayers, around 6 am, I would hurry to get some hot water and run back to get cold water from the well to have bearable bathing water. Most of the time, when I got to the queue by the well to get some cold water, though frustrating, my hot water would have turned cold.

At some point, I thought of another method with a friend. We fetched water before our 'light out' and hid it in the bush. Some other juniors did the same too. But to my surprise, the senior girls would wake up before 5 am, steal the water of the junior ones wherever it was hidden in the bush, and leave the empty bucket. It was frustrating to deal with. For me, this was torture of another kind. The sad part was that we could not tell anyone, and when we eventually mustered the courage to confront the senior girls, we were told that "This is life, and we have to get along with it."

These unpleasant events did not reduce the crisis but kept me out of class more often. Whenever my mother visited me, I would share my experiences with her while she would encourage me to endure. No one understood the pain, torture, and agony I went through in those days except God.

Despite my ordeal, the hostel still had its occasional enjoyable moments. I had to learn how to plait hair at the hostel. Any student who could not braid other people's hair would have no one to plait hers. Some students had to cut their hair because they did not want to learn how to plait.

I also learnt how to use hot coal iron. This requires caution as the coal iron could burn clothes within seconds. Some students would put their uniforms under their mattresses to 'bed iron' them. Another exciting experience was going to church in the local area. We would queue up in white dresses and the school's brown beret to differentiate us from other schools. The seniors often used that day to see their boyfriends who were from the nearby colleges, such as Anglican Boys High School and St. Finbarr's Secondary School.

A strange thing always happened in the hostel at midnight, particularly at the uncompleted building upstairs. I noticed that some students would go there to engage in some secret activities. We learnt that the seniors had a form of 'service' after 'light out' (this is after the light has been put off for us all to go to bed), but I never got involved.

After my first year and the irregular attendance at school due to my medical condition, the Principal invited my parents to discuss the way forward. The outcome of the discussion was that I would become a day student.

When I became a day student, my mother dropped me and picked me up at college. Once the route was mapped out, I found my way back home using public transport. On Wednesdays, we had extracurricular activities. I often thought of solutions to my health so that I could live a normal life. I knew my parents had tried their best, but I felt unfulfilled and looked for a solution. In my quest to find answers, I enrolled in the drama and cultural society. I participated in the Efik traditional dance and later joined the debating society. I also joined the Sports club, but I was not satisfied. I engaged in Art and Craft, where I made materials with tie and dye and domestic science, where I learnt how to bake.

Other responsibilities were attached to being a day student. I was expected to take care of my siblings, especially my younger brother. I had to make sure my younger brother got what he wanted. More so, he loved to be pampered. During my early secondary school days, my grandmother died, which affected me psychologically because I loved her. She told us stories from Tales by the Moonlight. She would cry whenever my parents wanted to beat me for being naughty. I enjoyed the little time I spent with her before she passed on to glory.

I joined the Scripture Union after a while. I attended the programme every Wednesday. There was a special programme where the guest speaker was Brother Kumuyi from the University of Lagos. I participated in the event, and after the sermon, there was an altar call. This was the moment I decided to follow Jesus Christ, and I remember telling myself that maybe I would be healed of this painful inherited disease. Thus, I went out, and the preacher prayed for me. Jesus Christ became the Saviour of my soul in August 1977. That event marked the beginning of my Christian journey. It sealed the promise that I would be free from premature death.

Due to the conviction in the Scripture Union, we were told to dress in moderation. No earrings or jewellery. You were to tie your scarf or use the school beret. Students were taught the scriptures and how to memorise them. This helped me a lot because, till today, I am guided by the word of God, and it has kept me going in life. My mother was the first to notice the changes in my mode of dressing.

My faith in Christ caused trouble between my parents and me. It had been a family tradition to take local herbal drinks for 'protection'. Apart from protection, it was also meant to make me do well in my studies. I was in a dilemma after I gave my life to Jesus. I was afraid of the consequences, so I took the herbal drink. I was scared of being beaten because years ago when I returned late from an errand to the market, I received the beating of a lifetime. I told myself that rejecting the herbal medicine would bring war. Each time I took it, I wept for betraying Jesus by not being bold enough to say no without minding the conse-quences. The tension was so high that I would pray and fast.

One fateful day, I told my mother that anyone in Christ did not need to take that herbal stuff for protection. Then she asked me why I took tablets for my illness, but I answered that God would heal me at the set time. I told God if I died after rejecting the herbal drink, He should receive me in His kingdom.

When it was time for the medicine to be administered, I said no, and hell broke loose. My mother reported me to my father immediately. My father never spoke much, but I was summoned to his room. He asked me why I declined the drink, and I explained my reasons. However, he said, "We serve Jesus too, and it is for protection." Then he told me to pack my belongings and get out if I refused to take the herbal drink. All my pleas fell on deaf ears.

I picked up a small suitcase and went to the back of our house, crying. After a while, he told my mother to let me into the house. I was thankful to God, thinking the battle had ended, having stood for my beliefs and conviction. But my mother would not take no for an answer. As soon as my father went out for his usual evening relaxation with his friends, my mother 'disciplined' me. Afterwards, I was at peace because Jesus gave me victory. From that day on, they stopped giving me herbal medicine.

I continued my studies as a day student, and after a while, I enrolled in an after-school studies programme. My siblings always followed me to the evening lesson. My younger brother came along because I had to take care of him. And he, in turn, loved it because it gave him an avenue to get out of the house. During this period, I led my immediate younger sister to Christ, and she accepted Jesus Christ as her Lord and Saviour.

Meanwhile, children of the upper class also attended the evening lesson. We would sit under the apple tree while our tutors, who we called big and small uncles, taught us. The success rate was high for those preparing to go into higher institutions. This lesson helped me in mathematics, especially using the "almighty formula" to solve algebra.

During that time, there were no mobile phones. We had to go to the Nigerian Telecommunications Limited (NITEL) to call anyone abroad. We could also use 'airmail blue paper' to post letters abroad. After my final O Level examinations, we travelled abroad for the summer holiday. My siblings returned to Lagos while I was left to continue my studies in the UK.

"And we know that all things work together for good to them that love God, to them who are the called according to his purpose"
Romans 8:28

CHAPTER 5

Coping With Life In The UK

Life in the United Kingdom was good, even though it took a while to adjust. The weather was not conducive for me. I stayed in the Isle of Wight, in Bembridge, for my A levels at a mixed school. In those days, the winter season was not easy to adjust to compared to this period of global warming. I had to start wearing trousers, which I objected to at first, and other essentials to keep my joints and body warm. I made enquiries about a Pentecostal church and got a church in Ryde. It was a friendly church, and a family adopted me for the period I was at college. I still communicate with this lovely family because they took me as one of their children. At the church, the youth often evangelised and ministered through songs. They also used guitar in their ministrations.

On Sundays, I found my way to the church and followed them home for dinner. In the evening, Uncle and Auntie Parker, as they were addressed, would drive me back to college. I told my adopted parents about my medical condition and what they should do when I have any crisis. I also gave them my parents' telephone number.

I had a wonderful time during my stay with them. I taught Auntie Ann the fundamental part of the Yoruba language and how to prepare Jollof rice, a Nigerian dish.

The doctors on the Island were not conversant with Sickle cell disease. When I had a crisis, the college called an ambulance, and I told them to contact my auntie before transfusing blood to me when they discovered that my blood level was low. Auntie passed the message to my parents, and they instructed her that no blood transfusion should be administered, just plenty of fluid and analgesic. It was in the hospital that I first noticed the denture used by older people in a glass of water where it was kept. The doctor discharged me eventually, and my parents visited me.

I attended a multicultural college as there were students from various parts of the world. At the hostel, we shared rooms with other races — Vietnamese, Chinese and English, among others. I was paired with a young Chinese lady, and we did get along. We both learnt a little of each other's native language.

Our meals were not just English dishes but consisted of diverse types of food. I preached Christ to those who showed interest, but the commitment was not there. Thus, no fellowship group was established at the boarding house. Two ladies from Zimbabwe followed me to Elim Pentecostal Church, and they were received with love. I did my water baptism by immersion with other youths of my age group at the church.

I visited the old people's homes in the summer and used the opportunity to tell them about God's love. I sang hymns to them, which they loved. The pain was usually severe during the cold weather, but God watched over me. My siblings and my first female cousin (now late) came for a holiday during the summer. They visited me on the Island where we went to places of interest like the Black Gang Chine.

My college was close to the sea, and it was lovely to see many people relaxing by the seashore. I never stayed long by the seaside because it was not palatable to my body system. College days were memorable, and studying was much more accessible and enjoyable.

My father later arranged that I should study business studies so I could manage his pharmaceutical business. I went to Oxford Secretarial College and did a Diploma in secretarial duties (Pitman). Life in Oxford was quiet as the environment was academically inclined. The few places of worship were Anglican and the Cathedral churches. Since I could not find a Pentecostal church, I attended an Anglican church, where I learnt many hymns whose lyrics I find helpful and encouraging till today. I lived with an elderly couple that accommodated other students, about three of us. We had breakfast and dinner together. We also talked about the events of the day. Life was not fun. My spiritual life was no longer on fire, and reading the bible was a struggle.

I marked my 21st birthday on a low key. My college mates came over to where I lived to celebrate with me. Although I was happy, I missed my family. I was delighted because I was not in crisis during that period but sad because I was not bubbling spiritually though I knew the light of God was there.

In my second year, my sister came for her A levels, and it was a relief to see a familiar face around. We always went out for meals whenever we had the opportunity. My sister had to live with a family, too. And during summer, our family would come around for a holiday.

During the half term, my father took me to some of his business associates in Geneva and Lugano in Switzerland. I felt a sense of belonging as he took me around as his secretary because my father hardly relates with his children.

After I had completed my course and I was satisfied with my shorthand speed, I decided to do a catering course — I had a passion for it. Besides, I had satisfied my parents by studying what they wanted me to study. When I informed my dad, he said, "I sent you to know what to do in the business world, not cook for me." That was the end of my passion for catering. He sent me to Bath for a crash course in Business Studies at Connaught College.

Meanwhile, in my quest for a pentecostal church, I discovered that there are several types of churches, and if one was not grounded in the word of God in the beginning, one could be led astray. I once went to a building and sat by the end of the pew. It felt like the gathering of the dead. Members were asked to talk to their loved ones. When I learned this was what the service was about, I never went there again. I met a man whom I thought was the 'marriageable' type. However, when I returned to Lagos, I thought otherwise because I desired a man who could make decisions on his own and was bold enough to admit his fault.

What lessons did I learn from my stay abroad?

My stay in the UK was filled with various levels of personal experiences. For instance, I learnt to be independent, to be firm with my decisions and to take responsibility for my actions — whether good or bad. I made some unpleasant decisions, but I learned from my mistakes.

CHAPTER 6
Life Back In Lagos

After spending a couple of years abroad, I returned to Nigeria. Things had changed at home, and the family had moved to my parents' house on Victoria Island. A posh place located where the crème de la crème of society lived. I was grateful to God for His hand over my parents' business.

I soon settled down in Lagos. I worked for my father as the Coordinator for Tanmo Pharmaceutical Ltd. Mum had always wanted me to work for my father. I also stood as his secretary whenever he was on business trips. I enjoyed working for my parents. My mother was working full time at the pharmaceutical company in Ikeja.

We would leave the house early in the morning and drive to Ikeja. Whenever either of them wanted to go early for work, I would follow them. And as weeks turned to months, I learned to find my way back home, especially when they had to do other things and I had to complete tasks assigned to me as a paid staff member.

My father was the leading distributor of a pharmaceutical product called Geriatric Pharmaton. He manufactured some other products, Tanmodol, Tamovita and more. My father and the company's sales representatives distributed to retailers in Lagos and other parts of Nigeria. He worked extremely hard, and his business blossomed.

Now that I was back in Nigeria, my pain and crisis had returned. And it was not pleasant at all. My mother would inject me with a strong painkiller called Novalgin, and it might take days for the pain to reduce. Consequently, this slowed down my work at the office. But then, I am glad that I worked for my parents because they understood they had to put up with my medical condition. I followed them to our family Anglican Church in Lagos. There, I learnt how to sing hymns in Yoruba. The church had evening services that were conducted in English, too.

After some time, I wondered if I would ever be free from this life of "leave home in the mornings, come back to do household chores (there was no house help in this new home), go to sleep and start all over the next day." On weekends, I did general cleaning with my siblings if they were not in the boarding school. I had no friends in Lagos. The ones abroad, I had to write to them because we did not have mobile phones in those days. You had to go to NITEL, which was quite stressful. I was not open to talking to either of my parents because they had created that fear in me when I was growing up, so I kept to myself.

However, one day I was bold enough to tell my mother that I was not happy with my life. I had no friends, and the country's epileptic power supply made things boring. I requested to attend an evening catering school. My mother agreed on the condition that anytime I returned home, I must finish the remaining housework.

I accepted to explore the world and even make new friends. I enquired about my next plan, and I enrolled for an evening catering class at Masha. I was glad when I was told that classes would be held once a week because it would have been unbearable if it were more than that due to my workload at home. It was a breather, and I was finally doing what I had always wanted to do.

On the first day of my catering class, I followed my mother to work, found my way from Ikeja to

Surulere and came back late in the evening. As the saying goes, there is no prize without pain. The task was quite demanding, especially on practical days when I had to take pots, baking tins and all other equipment along. But God strengthened me.

"Why catering?" you may ask. Catering had been on my mind for years. I wanted to learn how to bake and prepare different Nigerian dishes. During that phase, I understood that nothing comes free or easy in life; you must struggle and be determined to achieve your goals and I set out to do just that.

Along the line, I still prayed and studied the Bible, but the zeal was not as fervent as when I had the first love of Christ. I prayed for a partner, and God answered me. One sunny Saturday, I went to Tinubu Square in Lagos to view the fountain as well as do some shopping. I saw a picture of a father and mother with their two children — a son and daughter — on one of the postcards. I bought it and kept it in my Bible. I prayed regularly as I was desirous of my spouse and children. And I believed it would come to pass regardless of my health.

I went about my daily work at the office in addition to catering, cooking, and taking care of the home. I always attended church with my parents too. I was okay with this routine because I was not fond of partying. Whenever I came back late from my catering class due to transportation issues, I would find my house chores waiting for me. No one else would do them.

I yearned for freedom even as I continued to bear the unpleasant experiences until one fateful day. One evening after my catering class, I saw one of my former tutors who taught me lessons during my secondary school days (we called him small uncle). We exchanged pleasantries, and I took a cab home afterwards. Little did I know that the meeting was a divine appointment.

The catering course was for two years, and I had spent a year and a couple of months there. Then I met that same former lesson tutor at Masha roundabout again. This time around, we were able to talk at length. I asked him what he was doing at Masha, and he told me he was doing home lessons for some children in the area. He made enquiries about my marital status, among other things. He asked me to visit him at his residence, where he lived with his elder brother whom we addressed as Big Uncle (now late).

Months later, I finished my catering course and got my certificate. With my baking skills, I baked meat pies and sold them at the office. I felt terrific and fulfilled.

'Small uncle' and I began to date. I told my mother about it, but she felt it might not be a fruitful relationship. I knew he was just a churchgoer from the days he was my tutor, and he knew I was a devoted Christian since my secondary school days. He visited me at home one day, saw me in bandages and wondered what was wrong with me. I did not want to share my health issue with him because most of my friends in the past ran away from people with sickle cell. According to some of them, it was a life of continuous looking after and nursing their spouses. Well, our relationship grew stronger. He was looking for a good woman to be his wife, and I was looking for a man who would love me the way I was (in our dialect, it is called peki ko peki).

We went out together as young lovers do, and I eventually told him about my medical condition. When he said nothing, I wondered if he knew the gravity of the situation. All along, I left everything in the able hands of God. Indeed, life was tough, and you would see as matters unfolded. I had severe health challenges, although, on the surface, I was not different from other healthy ladies.

After a few months, my parents set the date of our wedding, and preparation was on top gear. I will forever be grateful to my father for his help. He supported me financially for antenatal care and delivery at one of the leading medical hospitals, Finnih Medical.

My husband did a series of tests to ascertain that his haemoglobin was positive and, to God's glory, his genotype was AA. This meant our glorious children would be AS, and there would not be any sickle cell in the family. After the tests, my husband said, "Sickle cell or not, I will not let you down." Those words would later serve as my succour during the wedding preparations and pregnancy.

Meanwhile, we both battled with pressure from our families. I had little to do or say about the wedding preparations. My parents did everything to their taste, and it was the talk of the 'circle of the big guns' in Lagos for a long time. On the engagement day, I saw my father weeping for the first time. It was a surprise to me because he rarely expressed emotions. That day, I felt something special in my spirit for my father.

The wedding day was colourful, and I remembered it for good. Although the ceremony made me tired, I was excited to have my freedom. There was a minor problem concerning accommodation. All my husband's efforts to secure a suitable accommodation proved abortive. Thus my parents allowed us to stay at our former abode.

My husband was from a low-income family. He was born and bred in the village. Even though he was not from a comfortable background like mine, I was not bothered. I stood my ground that no matter what happened, I had entered this commitment, and I loved him enough to stand by him.

At this point in my life, my spiritual walk was zigzaggy. The fire and zeal I had for Christ had become lukewarm after my studies at the Isle of Wight. In spite of this, I knew God's kindness was upon me. I also knew I was marrying a nominal Christian, but I thought it would be easy to make my husband give his life to Christ. However, this was not the case. No preacher converts unbelievers to God. Conversion is God's job as the Holy Spirit touches people's hearts to repent from their sins and accept to follow Jesus.

CHAPTER 7

My Married Life

When we had our first child, my mother came to stay with us. She did the daily bathing and care of the baby because I needed support in the early days of my delivery. After about a year, we got our accommodation.

The first five years of my marriage were a challenging period. Our children, a boy and a girl, were brilliant and delightful to nurture. They attended Yewande Memorial School, and they were academically sound. Our children loved visiting their grandparents at Victoria Island.

Within me, I was not fulfilled because my husband was not a born-again Christian. I always prayed and fasted so that God could touch his heart. We attended Chapel of the Healing Cross on Sundays, where the children were taught the Word of God in addition to the things I taught them about Jesus from the Bible.

Life continued, and my health was good to the glory of God. After church service one Sunday — it was New Year's Day — our car was nowhere to be found. We searched and searched but could not find it. We went to Radio Lagos so that details of the missing vehicle could be announced. My husband, being a teacher, also informed his students about it.

In the compound where we lived, I told a lady about the stolen car and asked if there was a Pentecostal church around because I needed firebrand prayers where my Spirit man would be stirred up for Christ. She understood and introduced me to Foursquare Gospel Church (FSGC) at Karimu. I went with the children, but my husband refused to follow us.

One Sunday, the sermon by Pastor Mrs Oshibanjo titled, "Wose, wose nbo" (the inspector is coming) ministered to my soul. After the sermon, I rededicated my life to Christ and be used for His glory even better than before. I felt relieved as an inner peace filled my soul.

Meanwhile, my husband had this habit of going out to drink. During one of such outings, he told me he heard some women saying that during one of the prayer meetings, prayers were raised for the family of a woman whose car had been stolen. While my husband neither smoked nor womanised, he loved to drink beer with his siblings. This habit continued for a while. Then, before the car was stolen, he would drop us at church and return to pick us.

Some weeks later, the mother church at Karimu announced the birth of another branch set up at Lawanson under the leadership of Pastor Omome. I was excited about this new development because it was just three minutes away from where we lived. That means I could attend church activities — vigil and evangelism, among others — easily. And I grew spiritually. Everything was according to God's divine plan because this new church was established when our car had been stolen. The Pastor encouraged me a lot concerning my husband, and we prayed, knowing God was in control of the situation. Not long after that, my husband's students informed him that they had seen our stolen car along an expressway. To God's glory, we recovered the vehicle.

On a particular Easter Sunday, the pastor made an altar call after the sermon, and I saw my husband at the front. He gave his life to Jesus Christ. The joy that filled my heart that day cannot be quantified. This began a new chapter of our Christian journey as a couple. He attended the Sunday school classes, the tenets of faith and bible study classes regularly.

All glory to God who is not slow in fulfilling His promises. Faithful is He who called me and strengthened me to trust Him as the anchor of our marriage. Do you think life would be rosy after this? No, it wasn't. That development opened another few years of trial, but I held on to Christ. Looking back at that phase, I can say that God's hand has always been upon my family.

Since we were now a family of Christ, the open space in the compound where we lived at Lawanson was used for a crusade meeting. Souls turned to the Lord, and many people in our local area came to the church.

We lived in that area for over eight years until the Landlord gave all the tenants a one-year quit notice. We looked for alternative accommodation. Our salary was not enough, and the Lagos State Government then did not pay teachers' salaries on time. At times, it takes two weeks into a new month to receive the previous month's salary. Our children attended private schools, and it was pretty challenging to make ends meet.

What my father had once told me was manifesting, but I believed then that although weeping may last for a night, joy will come in the morning, according to the word of God. It was more convenient living in Surulere because transportation was easily accessible. Healthwise, the Lord's hand was upon me. One of my uncles found a house help for me because fetching water and all other domestic shores coupled with office work were cumbersome.

In the ninth year, the property owner removed all the pipes leading to the soakaway in all the flats, thereby making life unbearable for all the tenants. Getting accommodation was not cheap. We had to sell some of our property to rent another flat, which was not within the commercial area. We rented a place at Ago Palace Way. There was electricity, and the environment seemed like a quiet place to live. However, before the lease expired, I regretted that we chose to live at the location. In fact, we realised that the agent had conned us. During the rainy season, the place was not motorable. We had to take public transport to take the children to school. Despite this, I continued attending church activities even if it took a pound of flesh because we prayed before moving to the new place.

During that time, I asked my father for a loan for some business, which he gave me willingly after negotiating the amount to pay him back monthly. My husband and I had carefully mapped out a plan. We set up a motorcycle business and took some classes on soap making business. The soap was called LADY B. Sales were coming in. People bought the soap, and returns also came in from the Okada business. We were able to repay the loan monthly as earlier agreed.

Although I was growing spiritually, the activities were telling on my health. I started to lose weight. After a while, my father became sick, and his business was no longer booming. This gave me a lot of concern. My mother had to take over the running of the company, and it was not easy for her.

My father gave his life to Christ

Words cannot describe how I felt when my father dedicated his life to God. He visited me one day, and I used the opportunity to talk to him about his salvation. He went to church regularly and was a chorister (he had such a good voice). He gave generously to the church and was a man with a large heart, but all of these without salvation would not earn him the Kingdom of God. I called my Pastor to conduct a deliverance service for him, and my father gave his life to Christ.

Although he could not stay long with us then because there was no electricity, and he was not comfortable in such an environment. As soon as he got back to the house, I liaised with my mother and my Pastor that all the mantle of the 'Freemason' should be disposed of. And she agreed with the plan.

Life continues

Our business was booming, and life was moving forward. Thieves came to the compound one day and fired gunshots, but, to the glory of God, nothing was stolen, and nobody was killed. However, I decided that we would no longer live in that area for safety reasons. My husband persuaded me, but I had prayed about it and made up my mind.

The children, the house help, and I moved to the storehouse at Lawanson, where my father received customers who needed pharmaceutical products. There was a room upstairs, and I informed my father about the situation. He allowed us to stay in the room. After the day's work in the evening, we slept upstairs. My husband could not stand living at Ago palace after a night by himself, so he joined us. We put cushions on the floor (we had sold all our furniture since there was no place to keep them). We sold most of our clothes too.

I never stopped committing the day into God's hands and asking the Holy Spirit to lead. I would wake the rest of the family for prayers, after which everyone would prepare for the day's job. We had an office cleaner who kept the environment clean from Mondays to Fridays.

Despite these changes in our lives, our church activities continued, and the children were able to work for the Lord. Memory verses from the Bible, recitations, and drama – to mention a few – became the norm. We continued with the soap business but had to stop the okada business because people were not faithful with the returns. My husband did private tutorials to boost the family income. Amid this hardship, God was faithful to me. I had no sickle cell crisis or panic attack. Meanwhile, my husband and our Pastor kept praying for a breakthrough.

One day, my father instructed my mother (although I believe my mother initiated the idea) to get me some money to renew my British passport and get the children's passports. Before this time, it had never occurred to me to take my family abroad. Besides, I did not want to be separated from my immediate family as I experienced growing up. When the necessary documents were ready, my mum said it was an opportunity to leave Nigeria for a greener pasture in London.

I was upset at first, but I could not say anything because I was at their mercy. They bought my ticket, including the children's, because I insisted on not leaving my children with them in Nigeria. Friends told me it would be difficult bringing my husband to the UK and that it might take years before the application would be granted. The day of our departure at Murtala Muhammed Airport was a sad sight. My mother accompanied us to the airport. The children were happy to get on the plane and consoled their dad and me. When we left, my husband vacated the apartment and went to stay with his cousin as we waited for what God would do for us.

"Take delight in the Lord,
and he will give you the desires of
your heart"
Psalm 37:4

CHAPTER 8

Life In The UK With The Children

My younger sister accommodated us in the UK. Since we did not know what the future had in store for us, we took a day at a time. Her family had to adjust to the new arrangement as three of us joined them in their two-bedroom flat. I felt as if I was invading their privacy even though her husband was a good in-law.

Before I left Nigeria, I went with the certificate of membership of Four-Square Gospel Church. So I contacted the London branch and fellowshipped there even though it was far from where we were living. I joined the prayer group and evangelism team in the Newham branch.

At my sister's house, the room where we slept was overcrowded. This was not good for her children and even for my health. A housing inspector came and noted that it was not fair on those children. Thus, six months after our arrival, an accommodation was allocated to us. In fact, it was a miracle, and I am forever grateful to God and my sister with her family, whom the Lord used on our arrival in the UK.

We have passed the first hurdle. Some members of the church came to bless the new home. I registered the children at a nearby school, and we adjusted to the new environment. I tried to get a clerical job but couldn't because I was not computer literate. I then applied for a jobseeker's allowance, which lightened the burden. It also allowed me to go back to school and do some courses. My husband and I communicated via letters, and when he had some money, he would go to the Nitel office to speak with us. This consumed a lot of money as mobile phones were not yet in vogue.

During one of our intercessory prayers, I told my prayer team members to join me in praying for a settlement visa for my husband, not a visiting visa. And we left it in God's hands to do what He alone can do best.

Back in Nigeria, my husband joined faith together with Pastor Omome and the believers at Lawanson Church in prayers. The Word of God says, "Ask anything in my name, and I will give you if you do not doubt." I read this part and saw it in a new light. It came to me that we cannot be praying without actions. So, I told my husband to file his papers for settlement and make sure his passport was valid. I also told him to inquire about the necessary documents needed at the Home office. Our prayer language changed to "what God has joined together, let no British law put asunder." It sounded silly, but we went ahead and we prayed along that line.

During this period, I was admitted to the hospital because of sickle pains. The stress of the happenings around me was getting to me. When I was discharged from the hospital, I tried to get a job to obtain payslips and go off the jobseeker's allowance. I did a night job for a few days but could not continue. At one point, I thought of applying for a loan from my bank, although my account had been dormant for years. But I knew all things were possible with God. I applied for the loan, reactivated my account, and got the loan. I took the loan because I did not want to approach anyone, especially my sister, who really tried for me.

A few days before my husband's visa interview in Lagos, I bought my travel ticket to Lagos. God took over the journey. There was no crisis regarding my health. It was a happy reunion with my mother and my husband. My husband and I went for the settlement visa interview. God was in action in the interview room. To my greatest surprise, the interviewer also flew from London on the same flight I was on the previous night. After we exchanged pleasantries, we got down to business. I was asked for my payslips and where I live. I had no job, and I lived in a government accommodation, so I told them the truth. I added that I was on Social Benefit due to health reasons. My heart was pounding, and I dared not raise my eyes to look at my husband. The officer analysed the implications behind my story. He said I was bringing someone to be a liability to the UK government since there was no evidence that I could support my husband.

The interviewer got up to consult with his team before giving the verdict. As we waited for his return, it felt like hours, even though it was just a few minutes. My husband and I could not say a word. The man returned and told us what the law said and that we did not meet the criteria. He said the government could not accommodate my husband because he would become a burden to the government housing council. He also said with my health condition, I did not need my husband to be in the UK before I got treatment.

When I heard this analysis, my heart fell. However, he said because of my marriage, which was over twelve years then, and the fact that our children needed a father figure in the home, our request would be granted. Since my husband had qualifications as a teacher, he would not be redundant concerning getting a job. In his words: "In the United Kingdom, we don't believe in breaking established families. Thus, your husband is granted indefinite leave to remain in the UK."

Immediately he said those words, my husband lifted me right in front of the interviewer. I could not believe my ears. We both thanked the man. When the man asked if we thought we would not get the approval, we said many had come out of the interview room in tears of sorrow.

That was yet another evidence that we serve a remarkable, faithful, and marvellous God. This testimony drew me even closer to God. Till today, I believe all things are possible. If it is according to His will and plan for our lives, it will surely come to pass. God is forever faithful to His Word and promises. He does not waver. Weeping may last for the night, but joy comes in the morning. Many people could not believe it, including my mother.

Some people even thought I was foolish for pressing forward in my marriage when they could not see any hope in sight. But the Lord did what no man could ever have done.

I returned to London ahead of my husband. He gave away some items and sold others to gather money for his trip. We were only temporarily separated for seven months. God was indeed faithful to us. And greater things He will do as we put our trust in Him.

God's faithfulness is new every morning. During our children's primary, secondary and university days in London, the hand of God was on them. They were obedient and disciplined and they worked in God's vineyard. We also encouraged them to learn musical instruments so they could use their gifts in the house of God.

I must admit that bringing up my children in the United Kingdom was a task that gave me joy because God took over their lives right from the beginning. It was a peaceful season for us as a family. We celebrated their successes. They were always cooperative. Although we had our moments of differences, I would not have asked for anything more because God Almighty is faithful. Now that our children are older, they take care of me in amazing ways.

I always knew that the heart of man is deceitful, even in places of worship. As I stated previously, some pastors and churches turn the hearts of children and even adults away from their families and "own" them. They fill these people with false doctrines and mess up their mindset. This is why the Word of God says the heart of a man is evil and desperately wicked. And God was mindful of our family in this aspect.

During the winter, the pain would be severe, and sometimes I was admitted to the hospital for observation under my consultant, Doctor R. Amos. But during those uncomfortable times, I was at peace, knowing my family was with me.

"I praise you, for I am fearfully and
wonderfully made.[a]
Wonderful are your works;
my soul knows it very well"
Psalm 139:14

CHAPTER 9

My Work Life

week after my husband settled in the UK, he found a job at McDonald's. He later got full-time employment at a Government Agency. I was off benefits and was living a typical working-class life. I got a job at Tesco as a pharmacy assistant due to the experience I had working for my father in Nigeria at his pharmaceutical company in Lagos for twelve years. I worked for my father for twelve years. From the Tesco pharmacy section, I applied for employment at the Department of Works and Pension, where I worked for twelve years uninterrupted.

I worked at different branches, but as I grew older, the pain from my health condition started to affect my mobility. My job was to attend to customers at the front desk, which adversely affected my health. Some of the customers were not polite, and this stressed me out. The management put me in the backroom as a Claim Processor Officer. The office also posted me to an office near my home.

At this new office, I noticed that staff members with different religious affiliations had a room for prayers. After seeking the face of God, I took courage and requested if Christians could also use the place for prayers. I got the permission, and we came together at an agreed time to pray for the establishment and other needs. These prayer sessions went on throughout my stay, and God answered our prayers. When I left, other believers did not have the eagerness to go on with the prayer time, and new workers were not encouraged.

During my years in the department of works and pension, my parents went to be with the Lord. I bless God that all their children are alive and living well. There was a moment of sibling rivalry, but God intervened. If God were not moving on our behalf, things would have been worse.

Dear reader, life comes with a series of tribulations. For me, it was different episodes of pain. For others, it might differ. However, the way you handle the storm will determine the outcome. You either handle it with prayers or bitterness.

Impact of Sickle cell anaemia on my job

I would have loved to work until my retirement age, but the crisis pains and reduced mobility affected my productivity. One day, the management informed me that my sick absences were too much. They told me they could dismiss me, or I could opt for voluntary retirement. I made them understand that my health condition was not of my making, nor was it a deliberate act. The management went ahead to give me a dismissal letter. I did not accept their decision, so I appealed against it.

My husband and I prayed about it. We informed the Consultant at the hospital. It was a long battle with the management, but my doctor provided all the necessary medical reports and stated their implications. In the end, we won the battle. And the company converted the dismissal letter to Medical Retirement with full benefits. This was God fighting my battle after eleven years in the civil service without any break, suspension, or incrimination. And I can boldly sing, "I can see Him working in my favour, fighting all my battles, and bringing in my miracles, He will do what he says He will do."

Additional testimonies

God was not yet done with me. He gave me another medical victory. My consultant had referred me to the orthopaedic surgeon concerning the reduced mobility due to a hip problem. In 2007, I was told to come for a hip operation as soon as possible. I checked in with the surgeon to know if the process would free me from the pains I was going through due to sickle cell anaemia. The surgeon said no, but it would make me walk better.

I prayed to God again, as I had learnt to do in the time of need. I discussed my dilemma about the operation with my husband, but I had the final decision to either do the procedure or not. After a while, I told the surgeon to keep an eye on my hip. To the glory of God, this is the eleventh year that I have been without the operation.

I still attend church, participate in praise and worship, evangelise, take Sunday school classes and minister whenever I am called to do so. When I am unwell, my husband has always been supportive, and he drives me whenever I need to do some shopping to avoid the stress of driving by myself. God prepared him for me, and I am grateful to him.

At some point, after I retired, we needed to downsize our accommodation. It became a major issue because we could not get a buyer. The mortgage bankers said the house would be repossessed. The house was on the market for over a year and a half. We prayed and prayed, and it seemed as if heaven was shut against us from selling the property. When a buyer eventually turned up, the price was too poor. We could not go for it because we would be at a loss and homeless.

One early morning, the Spirit of God ministered to me. He told me to be anxious for nothing but to rejoice. I confirmed this from the Bible and found the word in 1 Thessalonians 5:16-18 and Romans 12:12.

> *"Rejoice evermore. Pray without ceasing. In everything give thanks: for this is the will of God in Christ Jesus concerning you."* 1 Thessalonians 5:16-18

> *"Rejoicing in hope; patient in tribulation; continuing instant in prayer."* Romans 12:12

Having read these verses, my husband and I started praising the Lord. The Holy Spirit revealed another strategy to market the property, and God surprised us. The asking price was not only met, but God also added extra thousands of pounds for us so we could testify of His goodness.

Now, I am over sixty years to the glory of God. None of my bones is broken; no blood transfusion, known as hydroxyurea usually taken by patients with sickle cell disease. God did it! Every day, I stand upon the promises of Jesus, the King of kings and Lord of lords. I have every reason to go to church and rejoice in His presence continually. This book is to let the world know that all things are possible with God. One of my favourite scripture verses, which has kept me going, is Psalm thirty-four.

The virtue of hard work

I learnt from experience that by nature, a lazy person would not have the zeal to go to the house of God. In my view, tiredness, as an excuse for not fellowshipping with other believers, is laziness and procrastination which is a thief of time. My upbringing did not give room for laziness. I was brought up with disciplined hands, which helped me in my matrimonial home. Cooking and bringing up the children were not a burden for me. Training the children, teaching them about God and taking them for music lessons gave me joy.

On Wednesdays, we held a Bible study called the Disciple of Christ fellowship in our house. I would always tidy up the house before people arrived for the fellowship. These meetings kept us spiritually alive. The women's fellowship is called the Blessed Women Christian Fellowship (BWCF). This was where I met a lovely woman, Christine, and we became close friends. We encouraged each other physically, morally, spiritually and in other areas of life. I nicknamed her Mama Willy.

"For we are God's handiwork, created
in Christ Jesus to do good works,
which God prepared in advance for us
to do"
Ephesians 2:10

CHAPTER 10
In All, I Am Grateful To God

Regardless of how long I have been serving the Lord or the new heights I attain with the help of God, I learn new things daily. The Holy Spirit teaches me as I move from glory to glory according to 2 Corinthians 3:18 —

> *But we all, with open face beholding as in a glass the glory of the Lord, are changed into the same image from glory to glory, even as by the Spirit of the Lord.*

God kept me alive, and I am at peace with my soul. I feel pain in my body occasionally, but God always raises a standard for my comfort. To have mental, spiritual, and physical strength, every believer must administer Holy Communion because it is vital in a believer's life.

If your faith is weak, pray and speak God's word into your situation as I have been doing all my life. Declare God's word into all areas of your life – finance, marriage, health, family and children. I do not doubt that God has healed me. Though I still feel the symptoms once in a while, the crisis no longer affects me weekly as it used to when I was younger, except when I am stressed out. For this, I give all glory to my Redeemer who lives.

One of God's great privileges to my husband and me was the grace to witness our son's wedding. Whenever I reflect on my life, my soul rejoices because God is indeed faithful. For giving me the grace to be present on my son's special day, despite all of the challenges I had encountered, I am thankful. The world thought I would die at a younger age or never witness my children's growth. But God had a different plan for my life.

During my son's wedding ceremony, God opened up heaven and demonstrated his move. All my siblings, extended family, and fellow brethren were present. What else can I say than it pays to serve God in spirit and truth? It also pays to be obedient to Him.

My son married a pleasant Chinese lady. The most beautiful aspect is that she is a Christian. She is born again, so she understands the language of the Kingdom. Praise God!

Life after retirement

After I retired from work, I was not comfortable simply sitting and resting at home. So I joined the above fifties' club to engage myself and interact with other people. I attend the knitting and crochet class. It gives me an avenue to talk to others and learn from the older ones. I made a new friend, Theresa. One day, she told me she loved the evangelical cap I usually put on and asked if I was truly a believer. She was excited to talk to me about Jesus, and not long after that, the class noticed our love for God. Most of them do not want to hear about Jesus, but we talk about Jesus to anyone who cares to listen.

There, I knitted and crocheted baby boots and blankets in anticipation of the arrival of our grandchildren. The Lord answered our prayers by blessing us with a handsome grandson.

Dear reader, I want to assure you that being diagnosed with sickle cell anaemia or any other sickness is not a death sentence. If Jesus Christ is the pilot of your life, you will see His move in your life in every season as He has done in my life. Philippians 4:13 states: "For I can do all things through Christ that gives me strength."

If you have sickle cell anaemia as I do, you can manage it with God's help. Keep your body warm at all times. Always drink plenty of water and have enough rest. Avoid smoking. Do regular but light exercises and massage with deep heat creams, heat pads or hot water bottles. In addition, be positive. Do not entertain negative thoughts. Don't allow your situation to weigh you down. Eat a healthy and balanced diet. Eat fruits and vegetables to avoid constipation from prescribed medications.

As long as you play your part and you religiously observe the suggestions, with God on your side, you will prevail. Many are the afflictions of the brethren, but if you trust in God and hold on to His covenant, He will never fail you.

The Author of life

Let me tell you about the person who has brought me this far. It is no other person but the author of life, God Almighty, the creator of heaven and earth. He created us in His image. As written in Genesis, God created man after His likeness. He placed Adam and Eve in the Garden of Eden to till the land. He said, "Be fruitful and multiply", but man disobeyed God's instructions. Man followed his selfish desires by obeying the enemy, Satan.

Take note of the following:

(a) Satan deceived man. Thus, evil and wickedness entered the world. Man's disobedience separated him from God because God cannot behold sin. However, God made the first move to reconcile man back to himself. So that man could live a life pleasing unto God, He sent His only begotten Son to be the perfect sacrifice to wash away man's sin. Jesus Christ shed His blood for you and me on the cross. God loves us so much that Jesus Christ became the perfect atonement for our disobedience. He willingly laid His life to be slain for us because without the shedding of blood, there is no forgiveness of sins Hebrews 9:22.

(b) Only the blood of Jesus can wash away our sins. Once you believe by faith that Jesus Christ is truly the Son of God and that He died for your sins on the cross of Calvary, you are forgiven. Unless you believe that He died and rose again and that He is alive forever, only then can you have Eternal life. Jesus laid down His life as a perfect sacrifice to wash away our sins. The blood of bulls and rams could not wash our sins away (Hebrews 10:4). Only a sinless man can do that, and that man is Jesus, who was born of virgin Mary into this world of sin. Jesus has paved the way for us because He is the Way, the Truth, and the Life John 14:6.

(c) The road that leads to eternal destruction in hellfire, where Satan and his demons dwell, is broad. But narrow is the road that leads to eternal life in heaven, the home for those who believe and accept Jesus Christ as their Lord and Saviour Matthew 7:13-14.

(d) God does not ask you for money or any other thing rather than your faith. He wants you to acknowledge that you are a sinner. He will forgive your sins when you confess them and accept Jesus as your Lord and Saviour. Works of righteousness will not give you passage to eternal life but God's grace alone. He is calling you today to leave the path of sin and turn to Him.

Invite the Lord Jesus Christ into your life to be your Saviour. Confess your sins to Him and tell Him how sorry you are. He will forgive you and write your name in the Book of Life. Amen. Jesus Christ is the only one who can give you inner peace in this world of violence, hatred, and sin. Give Him access to every area of your life (without restriction), and trust Him in whatever you may be going through.

God is not a magician, but He blesses those who trust and obey Him. According to Psalm 30:5,

"For his anger endureth but a moment; in his favour is life: weeping may endure for a night, but joy cometh in the morning." Have faith.

The bottom line is, "if you confess with your mouth the Lord Jesus Christ and believe in your heart that God raised Him from the dead, you will be saved; for with the heart, one believes unto righteousness, and with the mouth, confession is made unto salvation Romans 10:10. Once you have done this, you are born again.

"Jesus answered and said unto him, Verily, verily, I say unto thee, Except a man be born again, he cannot see the kingdom of God" John 3:3. Now that you are born again, begin to claim God's promises upon your life as I did in my life. The moment you invite Jesus Christ into your life, the Holy Spirit will come upon you. But note that the Holy Spirit is a gentleman and will not force Himself on you. If you give Him permission to rule and reign in every department of your life, He will help you. Prayerfully ask God to lead you to a bible believing church where the uncompromising word of truth is preached daily.

As I journey on in life, by the grace of God, I will continue to trust and obey Him. I will continue to pray, intercede, worship, and evangelise until Jesus returns to rapture His own or calls me home.

"The Lord is not slack concerning his promise, as some men count slackness; but is longsuffering to us-ward, not willing that any should perish, but that all should come to repentance. But the day of the Lord will come as a thief in the night; in which the heavens shall pass away with a great noise, and the elements shall melt with fervent heat, the earth also and the works that are therein shall be burned up." 2 Peter 3:9-10

Affirm these words with me:

This is not my final bus stop. The best is yet to come because God has greater plans for my life. Hallelujah! I am a work in progress in the hand of my faithful Lord Jesus Christ, a tool for the Master's use. Amen.

"Therefore, my beloved brethren, be steadfast, immovable, always abounding in the work of the Lord, knowing that your labour is not in vain in the LORD."

1 Corinthians 15:58

One of my favourite choruses

Let others see Jesus in you (2x)
Keep telling the story,
Be faithful and true,
Let others see Jesus in you.

MARANATHA
Revelation 22:20

References on medical information (Fig. 1 Page 18):
Homerton University Hospital (NHS Foundation
Trust) Haematology Department (RJA/1.7.05 revised
14.5.09.)

www.sickell.org/whatistext2.htm leaflet

Diagram on page 20 courtesy of Minister Shepherd
Emmanuel Alade of Pleasant Surprise Church
International

Inspirations from:
"Insight for living" by Pastor Charles Swindoll
"Leading the Way" by Pastor Michael Youssef

Scripture References (page 83 - 84)
a. Genesis 1 & 2 (creation story)
b. John 3:16
c. John 14:6
d. Matthew 7:13-14

Printed in Great Britain
by Amazon